I'M ANOINTED BECAUSE...

COURAGE TO SURRENDER

RONALD KISAAKYE
&
TONYA BRUCE

Copyright © 2025 by Tonya Bruce.

ISBN (eBook): 979-8-9907638-9-0
ISBN (softcover): 978-1-968012-00-7
ISBN (hardcover): 978-1-968012-44-1

Library Of Congress Catalog Card Number: 2025909923

All rights reserved. No part of this book may be reproduced or transmitted in any form or by any means, electronic or mechanical, including photocopying, recording, or by any information storage and retrieval system without express written permission from the author, except in the case of brief quotations embodied in critical reviews and certain other noncommercial uses permitted by copyright law.

Published in the United States of America by:
Lynx Publishers

The evil things now have become normal and acceptable in modern society

—King Victor Williams

PREFACE

I'm Anointed Because... is more than a personal testimony—it is a spiritual call to surrender, to believe, and to wait patiently on God's miraculous timing. These pages were written to inspire transformation, hope, and deeper faith, especially in a world that often feels uncertain and disconnected from truth.

Already, the message has begun to impact lives. One early reader from Uganda shared how the book affirmed his faith and brought encouragement to his family. He was especially touched by the story of Mrs. Jennifer a woman healed and called into ministry whose journey became a testimony of God's power and purpose.

This book is for anyone longing to experience the fullness of God's promises. Whether you are waiting on a miracle, facing a storm, or simply seeking direction, may these reflections remind you that your anointing is not in your strength, but in your surrender.

Let this be your invitation to trust Him more deeply, and to discover that breakthrough begins at the moment of complete submission.

—***King Victor Williams***

CONTENTS

INTRODUCTION 1

CHAPTER 1 3

   IT ALL BEGINS FROM THE CROSS 4

CHAPTER 2 6

   ACCEPTING JESUS CHRIST AS YOUR PERSONAL SAVIOUR 7

   PERSONAL SAVIOUR 9

CHAPTER 3 14

   KNOWING HIS SUPREMACY 15

     1. CHANGING OUR ATTITUDE 16

     2. FAITH 17

     3. ENDURING 18

CONCLUSION 19

IM ANOINTED BECAUSE...

INTRODUCTION

For now, I may not have the potential at this point of time to build colleges in every country, or hospitals in every state to teach and dress up your wounds but I believe through this book, you're to find the right answer.

I praise God because you have a chance of reading or hearing the secrets of God. This is the right time and I believe God has a big plan for your life.

This book will help transform your life, it will lead you to the right path of getting close to and knowing the good plans of God for you.

Through submission to surrender our Lord Jesus Christ, there is joy, peace, freedom and abundant life so brethren, I don't want to see any one missing any of these.

Through my eyes as a Christian believer, I have seen this world continuously changing, and I believe the natural world is unsettled.

Many people have lost their lives and assets due to the rise of different diseases, financial crises, wars among nations, relational struggles, and many other factors.

All these have not just happened today. All these have been going on since the early age of the universe. But as Christians, Jesus has called us to settle the storm and overcome every challenge through Him.

CHAPTER 1

RONALD KISAAKYE & TONYA BRUCE

IT ALL BEGINS FROM THE CROSS

Since sin entered the garden of Eden these problems have existed. But God has provided a way to overcome them (According to the generation).

In the Old Testament, we see different generations facing all these challenges due to the disobedience of men to God. Good Bible readers can remember the seasons of Noah, the city of Sodom and Gomorrah, the slavery of Israelites in Egypt, and the rising and falling of various kingdoms.

But God had a plan from the beginning to settle (redeem) the world. Because He loves man so much, God gave His one and only son to die for our sins on the cross, and whoever believes in Him (Jesus) shall not perish but have eternal life. (John 3:16)

IM ANOINTED BECAUSE...

As every journey must have a starting point, God also built a plan to save man. Because His plans are good for us, God sent Jesus to die to pay for our sins and rebellion. Jesus was beaten so we could be whole. All of us, like sheep, have strayed away; we have left God's path to follow our own, yet the LORD laid on him the sins of us all. (Isaiah 53:4-5)

Jesus Christ carried our sins in His body on the cross so that we could be freed from our sins. We could live a life that has God's approval. Through Jesus we have the ability to have a covering of grace and mercy that God sees us righteous and holy.

Jesus' wounds have healed you. (1 Peter 2:24). God's mission is to save all men through His son Jesus Christ. This was fulfilled through Jesus' death on the cross and resurrection from the dead. There is now no judgement or condemnation against anyone who believes in him. (Romans 8:1)

CHAPTER 2

IM ANOINTED BECAUSE...

ACCEPTING JESUS CHRIST AS YOUR PERSONAL SAVIOUR

I have moved to many areas for missionary work, preaching and teaching people about the good news of our Lord Jesus Christ. I have faced one constant challenge in all these areas. It is that many people falsely believe they are in a right relationship with God.

The only way to enter the family of God is to confess your need for Him. Second, recognize you are a sinner and you need forgiveness. Third, to believe that his forgiveness is only available through believing in His only son Jesus Christ, who gave His life for us on the cross. (Romans 3:23-24)

Through believing this in your heart and by openly declaring your faith that you're saved, you are made right with God. (Romans 9:10)

RONALD KISAAKYE & TONYA BRUCE

It's really very hard in this generation for a man to believe that he is a sinner and needs forgiveness from God. This is because society has changed and things that were once seen as being evil are now regarded as acceptable behavior. We can see this in dressing, songs people sing and lifestyles. But God's standard as far as sin is concerned has never changed. One should not consider only deeds like murder, stealing or committing adultery as sins. Even being unfaithful, witnessing falsely or misusing the name of the Lord are also sins. Bible readers, you can recall the commandments God gave to Moses in the desert. (Exodus 20:1-17)

Since the beginning of mankind's journey on this earth, we have been thinking we know better than the Creator. Then we end up trying to do things our own way in our own strength. This is where we lack the power to change ourself or the circumstances that are temporary uncomfortable. Doing our own thing is not only described as sin but also declares that we're all guilty.

IM ANOINTED BECAUSE...

PERSONAL SAVIOUR

Take a minute to think of the power of Jesus Christ demonstrated through great miracles He did in the Bible. Think about that person who has told you what God's miracles has done in their life. I believe you have forgotten that Jesus is more than ready to save you from any challenge that is crossing your path today. Jesus can set you free from any obstacles in your way. The decision is before you. It's a call to every single Christian, like it or not.

If we have accepted the salvation Jesus offers, we are called to live in submission to His Lordship. Submission means you choose to surrender everything in your life, even life itself. This could be your business, family, ministry, friends and any life innovations. This means you have to put yourself in the position of having no choice but to go to Jesus to lead your life. This also means that for every challenge that comes our way, He is responsible. Remember He is a Supreme Savior.

It's hard for human beings to submit everything to Jesus Christ. In human knowledge and capacity, it's really hard. But it's not impossible, with God all things are possible. (Matt 19:23)

Surrender is only one part of the process, submission is a lifelong active part of the Christian life. Even surrendering was an act of submission to the call of the Holy Spirit at the moment we believed and reconciled us to the Father. The power to overcome one's will is power that comes from God. Once we believe and accept Jesus Christ, God gives us His Holy Spirit to guide and teach us all things. This is the power, the anointing that we act in submission to God's word. It's by His grace and holiness that we have this great Love from the Father.

To put this in other words, Surrender is an act of submission to the call of the Holy Spirit who desires to reconcile us to God the Father.

IM ANOINTED BECAUSE...

Many people think that accepting Jesus will stop or limit challenges from coming into their lives, I say, challenges do keep coming even after salvation. The only difference is that we overcome them through and power of the Holy Spirit that God placed in us when we accepted Jesus Christ as our Lord. (Psalms 34: 19-20)

Christians, we must let the Holy Spirit guide us and accept His teaching if we are to enjoy the goodness of God. We can no longer do things in our own power. As the earthly world desires freedom and happiness, they are left with disappointment, blame, shame, and bondage. When we believe in Jesus, submit our lives and our wills to God, we become slaves to the Holy Spirit. Then we are able to enjoy the freedom God gives. God promises we will have internal life with Him in heaven.

In December 2009, my mom fell sick and was admitted to Nakaseke Hospital. Doctors performed abdominal surgery on her. After a few weeks we came back home. There was no change at all. She then was admitted to Mulago Hospital where doctors said she had intestinal cancer. We were facing a difficult situation as a family. We had no money, and my dad was puzzled. For over seven days she continued to get increasingly worse because we had no money for medication. Mom came back home and I stopped studying. One evening, Mum called me to take a floor mat and pillow to church with her. She felt ready to die. She said if I'm to die, I want to die in Church. I heard her praying, "My Father in Heaven, I have come before you. No doctor can save me nor my friends, but you hear me. If you want me to live, I will tell the world that you're my healer and so I will give you my life."

By then, mom was 38kgs (84 lbs.). After submitting and gaining faith in our Lord Jesus Christ, mom started to eat salt and fats. She is now very healthy weighing 94kgs (206 lbs.). She is preaching the gospel in Uganda. The life of Nassazi Jenepher was completely changed, physically and spiritually by surrendering and submission to God.

IM ANOINTED BECAUSE...

God knows your situation and He understands when you get stuck. He knows how much we need His help. The problem is we don't give Him a chance to work in our lives. Many Christian think that God will just come and make physical miracles in their lives. Sometimes He does that and sometimes He gives us His wisdom and His power to overcome our problems. See our problems and circumstances are opportunities to glorify Him and this demonstrate our submission and surrender to the world.

Stop for a moment, close your eyes, tell God you are surrendering and submitting your life and WILL over to His care. Ask the Holy Spirit to guide you now, right now. Take more than a few minutes to listen.

CHAPTER 3

IM ANOINTED BECAUSE...

KNOWING HIS SUPREMACY

Through my gospel missions, I have visited many different churches. People have come to me with various questions:

1. Does Jesus have the power to overcome my challenge?
2. Really, does Jesus care for me?

I have a good answer for everyone with such questions: **YES**

Many times back when I got puzzled, I would go to bars and drink beer and chill with old friends. I used to play pool and have fun with beautiful ladies in the bars. I had questions in life like you. But one time in the morning while seated on my bed alone in my room, the Holy Spirit asked me "Do you know how much God loves you? And do you realize His good plans for you?"

On that day, I had nothing to eat because I had no money. But after the Holy Spirit spoke to me, I gained courage, and my life changed.

Many Christians get confused in understanding the Power of God. There are spiritual things a man should consider to discover the supremacy of God:

1. CHANGING OUR ATTITUDE

We have to realize that trials are part of our lives. (Romans 8:20-21). Our need is a necessary step in His redemption plan. So God allows trials in our lives so that we can seek Him.

When trials come, how do you control your attitude? Don't let your attitude be a problem to yourself due to the trial you're facing. Just praise God; He is lifting you to the next level.

You are not alone in the trial, "No," God is always with you. He will support and guide you to overcome it, like Daniel in the den of lions.

Don't ask yourself "why" "why me?" "Why are all these things happening to me?"

Just surrender and submit to ask the Holy Spirit what to do and He will come up with the right answer to overcome the trial. This will be a much better plan than you could have thought of yourself, I promise.

2. FAITH

To receive wisdom, knowledge and power from God you must submit and surrender. You also need faith. You must believe in and have faith in our Lord Jesus Christ. We express our faith to the world by our actions. God's word says, faith without action is dead. (James 2:13-26)

As here we're seeking to understand the supremacy of our Lord, we must use every opportunity that comes our way with faith. With all the miracles Jesus preformed in the New Testament, He encouraged faith and action to the people and their lives were transformed.

He asked: Do you want to be healed?

He said: Rise up and move...

TO EXERCISE THE POWER OF OUR LORD JESUS CHRIST WE MUST NOT DOUBT BUT HAVE LIVING FAITH IN HIM.

3. ENDURANCE

Once you declare that your future is His, your money is His, your family is His, and your entire life is His, you stand in the position of being a disciple no matter what the circumstance. This means you are positioned to receive everything you need from Him. But as challenges come our way, we must walk by faith in Jesus Christ our Lord, this is how we overcome our circumstances.

Enduring means to keep on going however strong the storm is. Standing and relying on the wisdom and the Word of God, before you make a move (step).

There are some moments when we feel like giving up, when the discouragements are around us, and problems look enormous. Please don't think of surrendering, just ask God to show you the right Path of His will.

CONCLUSION

Therefore, brethren, do not lose hope in our Lord Jesus Christ. Always stand firm, no matter how great the challenge may seem, because just when you least expect it, the Lord will show up. He will come your way with bigger and better plans. You will begin to see that while others may be facing even greater difficulties, God has placed you in a position of strength—to grow rich in faith, even more than those living in ease and comfort.

As Christians, we must remain faithful to our calling. Do not give up. Do not give in to temptation. Do not throw in the towel on the assignment God has given you—even when it gets tough. Our Lord Jesus Christ will reward you in due time!

www.ingramcontent.com/pod-product-compliance
Lightning Source LLC
Chambersburg PA
CBHW070051070426
42449CB00012BA/3235